Great Start!

Purchased with
Smart Start Funds

The Meat and Protein Group

by Helen Frost

Consulting Editor: Gail Saunders-Smith, Ph.D.

Consultant: Linda Hathaway
Health Educator
McMillen Center for Health Education

Pebble Books

an imprint of Capstone Press
Mankato, Minnesota

Pebble Books are published by Capstone Press
151 Good Counsel Drive, P.O. Box 669, Mankato, Minnesota 56002
http://www.capstone-press.com

1 2 3 4 5 6 05 04 03 02 01 00

Library of Congress Cataloging-in-Publication Data
Frost, Helen, 1949–
    The meat and protein group/by Helen Frost.
    p. cm.—(The food guide pyramid)
    Includes bibliographical references and index.
    Summary: Simple text and photographs present the foods that are part of the
meat and protein group and their nutritional importance.
    ISBN 0-7368-0539-7
    1. Nutrition—Juvenile literature. 2. Food—Juvenile literature. [1. Food. 2. Meat.
3. Nutrition.] I. Title. II. Series.
TX355.F775 2000
613.2—dc21   99-047744

Note to Parents and Teachers

The Food Guide Pyramid series supports national science standards related to physical health and nutrition. This book describes and illustrates the meat and protein group. The photographs support early readers in understanding the text. The repetition of words and phrases helps early readers learn new words. This book also introduces early readers to subject-specific vocabulary words, which are defined in the Words to Know section. Early readers may need assistance to read some words and to use the Table of Contents, Words to Know, Read More, Internet Sites, and Index/Word List sections of the book.

Table of Contents

The Food Guide Pyramid 5

The Meat and Protein Group . . . 7

Kinds of Meat and Protein 9

Servings and Energy 21

Words to Know 22

Read More 23

Internet Sites 23

Index/Word List 24

4

The food guide pyramid shows the foods you need to stay healthy. The meat and protein group is near the top of the food guide pyramid.

Meat is the part of an animal that people eat. Protein is found in all plants and animals.

Beef is in the
meat and protein group.

Chicken is in the
meat and protein group.

Sea Trout
Fillet
$3.50
A lb.

Fresh
Haddock
$4.50
A lb.

Whitting Fille
$3.25
A lb.

12

Fish is in the
meat and protein group.

Eggs are in the
meat and protein group.

Nuts are in the
meat and protein group.

Peanut butter is in the
meat and protein group.

You need two to three servings from the meat and protein group every day. Meat and protein make you strong and give you energy.

Words to Know

food guide pyramid—a triangle split into six areas to show the different foods people need; a pyramid is big at the bottom and small at the top; people need more food from the bottom of the food guide pyramid than from the top.

meat—the part of an animal that people eat; beef, chicken, and fish are kinds of meat.

protein—a substance found in all plants and animals; meat, cheese, eggs, beans, nuts, and fish are good sources of protein.

serving—a helping of food or drink; one serving from the meat group is 2 to 3 ounces (55 to 70 grams) of cooked meat or fish, 1 egg, 1/2 cup (125 grams) of cooked dried beans, 2 tablespoons (30 ml) of seeds or nuts, or 2 tablespoons (30 ml) of peanut butter.

Read More

Frost, Helen. *Eating Right.* The Food Guide Pyramid. Mankato, Minn.: Pebble Books, 2000.

Kalbacken, Joan. *The Food Pyramid.* A True Book. New York: Children's Press, 1998.

Powell, Jillian. *Fish.* Everyone Eats. Austin, Texas: Raintree Steck-Vaughn, 1997.

Internet Sites

Eggs and Good Health
http://www.aeb.org/food/eggs-health.html

Food Guide Pyramid
http://www.kidshealth.org/kid/food/pyramid.html

Food Guide Pyramid Game
http://www.nppc.org/cgi-bin/pyramid

Food Pyramid: Meat, Poultry, Fish, Dry Beans, Eggs, and Nuts
http://www.ganesa.com:80/food/meat.html

Index/Word List

animal, 7
beef, 9
chicken, 11
eat, 7
eggs, 15
energy, 21
fish, 13
food, 5

food guide pyramid, 5
healthy, 5
nuts, 17
peanut butter, 19
people, 7
plants, 7
servings, 21
strong, 21

Word Count: 117
Early-Intervention Level: 10

Editorial Credits

Mari C. Schuh, editor; Heather Kindseth, cover designer; Sara A. Sinnard, illustrator; Kia Bielke, illustrator; Kimberly Danger, photo researcher

Photo Credits

David F. Clobes, 1, 10
Frances M. Roberts, 20
Gregg R. Andersen, cover, 6
International Stock/R. Pharaoh, 14
Jack Glisson, 18
Photophile/Matt Lindsay, 12
Unicorn Stock Photos/Eric R. Berndt, 16
Visuals Unlimited/Arthur Hill, 8